CREATING
AFFLUENCE

DEEPAK CHOPRA

CREATING AFFLUENCE

The A-to-Z Steps to a Richer Life

FOREWORD BY RICHARD CARLSON

AMBER-ALLEN PUBLISHING
NEW WORLD LIBRARY
SAN RAFAEL, CALIFORNIA

© 1993 Deepak Chopra, M.D.
© 1998 Deepak Chopra, M.D.

Based on the original audio production © 1992 by Quantum Publications, Inc.

Co-published by Amber-Allen Publishing and New World Library

Editorial Office:	Distribution Office:
Amber-Allen Publishing	New World Library
P.O. Box 6657	14 Pamaron Way
San Rafael, CA 94903	Novato, CA 94949

Editorial and production: Janet Mills
Cover and text design: Beth Hansen-Winter
Cover illustration: Chantal Saperstein

Library of Congress Cataloging-in-Publication Data

Chopra, Deepak.
    Creating affluence : the a-to-z steps to a richer life / [Deepak Chopra]

      p. cm.
    1. Wealth—Miscellanea. 2. Wealth—Psychological aspects. 3.
Transcendental Meditation. I. Title.
    HB251.C48 1993
    330. 1'6—dc20   93-27861
                                           CIP

ISBN 1-880032-42-2 (hardcover)
ISBN 1-878424-34-3 (paperback)
ISBN 13 : 978-1-878424-34-1
Printed in Canada on acid-free paper
Distributed by Publishers Group West

20 19 18

DEDICATION

*To all those who give of themselves,
and in their giving receive the lavish abundance
of the universe.*

. . . .

AFFLUENCE, *unboundedness, and abundance*
are our natural state.
We just need to restore the memory
of what we already know.

CONTENTS

. . . .

FOREWORD

*W*ealth consciousness is so much more than simply having the ability to make money. It's a mind-set that involves seeing life, not as a struggle, but as a magical adventure where our needs are met with grace and ease. It includes the ability to see beauty wherever you go, to have gratitude as your primary emotion and an open heart to all you meet. Wealth consciousness is a state of mind, a sense, not of believing, but really *knowing* that what we need is available to us.

As Deepak clearly demonstrates in this remarkable little book, affluence is indeed our natural state of being. He shares with us specific tips that assist us in tapping into this unlimited potential. As I read through the wisdom contained in these pages I was struck by the fact that, to the extent that I have created affluence in my own life, I have done so by these very same principles; they are universal. I'm confident in my prediction that, should you read this book and take to heart the steps that are clearly laid out, you will discover that life is easier and more abundant than you ever thought possible. I send you my love and best wishes.

Treasure the gift of life,

Richard Carlson

author of *Don't Sweat the Small Stuff*

INTRODUCTION

*O*nce upon a time in a far-away land, a young man went to the forest and said to his spiritual master, "I want to have unlimited wealth, and with that unlimited wealth, I want to help and heal the world. Will you please tell me the secret to creating affluence?"

And the spiritual master replied, "There are two Goddesses that reside in the heart of every human being. Everybody is deeply in love with these supreme beings. But there is a certain secret that you need to know, and I will tell you what it is.

"Although you love both Goddesses, you must pay more attention to one of them. She is the Goddess of Knowledge, and her name is Sarasvati. Pursue her, love her, and give her your attention. The other Goddess, whose name is Lakshmi, is the Goddess of Wealth. When you pay more attention to Sarasvati, Lakshmi will become extremely jealous and pay more attention to you. The more you seek the Goddess of Knowledge, the more the Goddess of Wealth will seek you. She will follow you wherever you go and never leave you. And the wealth you desire will be yours forever."

. . . .

There is power in knowledge, desire, and spirit. And this power within you is the key to creating affluence.

A NOTE
FROM THE AUTHOR

The material in this book is extremely concentrated and has to be literally metabolized and experienced in the consciousness of the reader.

For best results, I suggest that you read the entire book once and subsequently read five pages on a daily basis. Upon completing the book, start again.

Make this a lifelong habit, and wealth in all its forms will follow you wherever you go.

Infinite worlds appear and disappear in the vast expanse of my own consciousness, like motes of dust dancing in a beam of light.

— Ancient Vedic Saying

PART I

Creating Affluence

CHAPTER 1

The Source of All Abundance

Affluence is the experience in which our needs are easily met and our desires spontaneously fulfilled. We feel joy, health, happiness, and vitality in every moment of our existence.

Affluence is reality, and the true purpose of this book is to give us an insight into the nature of reality.

When we are grounded in the nature of reality and we also know that this same reality is our own nature, then we realize that we can create anything, because all of material creation has the same origin. Nature goes to the same place to create a cluster of nebulas, a galaxy of stars, a rain forest, or a human body as it goes to create a thought.

All of material creation, everything that we can see, touch, hear, taste, or smell is made from the same stuff and comes from the same source. Experiential knowledge of this fact gives us the ability to fulfill any desire we have, acquire any material object we want, and experience fulfillment and happiness to any extent we aspire.

The principles expressed in this book relate specifically to the creation of unlimited material wealth, but these principles can be applied to fulfill any desire, because they are the same principles that nature uses to create material reality out of a nonmaterial essence.

Before we go into these principles, I would like to discuss in a little detail what science, and particularly physics, has to say about the nature of this universe we live in, the nature of our human bodies, the nature of our minds, and the relationship of all these to each other.

. . . .

According to quantum field theorists, all material things — whether they are automobiles, human bodies, or dollar bills — are made up of atoms. These atoms are made up of subatomic particles which, in turn, are fluctuations of energy and information in a huge void of energy and information.

Elsewhere in my books and tapes I have explored in detail the nature of quantum reality. Without going into detail, the basic conclusion of quantum field theorists is that the raw material of the world is nonmaterial; the essential stuff of the universe is nonstuff. All of our technology is based on this fact. And this is the climactic overthrow of the superstition of materialism today.

Fax machines, computers, radios, television — all these technologies are possible because scientists no longer believe that the atom, which is the basic unit of matter, is a solid entity. An atom is not a solid entity at all; it is a hierarchy of states of information and energy in a void of all possible states of information and energy.

The difference between one material thing and another

material thing — for example, the difference between an atom of lead or an atom of gold — is not on the material level. The subatomic particles such as protons, electrons, quarks, and bosons that make up an atom of gold or lead are exactly the same. Moreover, although we call them particles, they are not material things; they are impulses of energy and information. What makes gold different from lead is the *arrangement* and *quantity* of these impulses of energy and information.

All of material creation is structured out of information and energy. All quantum events are basically fluctuations of energy and information. And these impulses of energy and information are the nonstuff that make up everything that we consider stuff or matter. So it becomes clear that not only is the essential stuff of the universe nonstuff, but that it is *thinking* nonstuff. For what else is a thought but an impulse of energy and information?

We think of thoughts as occurring only in our head, but that is because we experience them as linguistically structured thought that is verbally elite and speaks to us in the English language — in my case, with an Indian accent. But those same impulses of energy and information that we experience as thoughts — those *same impulses* — are the raw material of the universe.

The only difference between thoughts inside my head and those outside my head is that I experience thoughts inside my head in linguistically structured terms. But before a thought becomes verbal and is experienced as language, it is just an intention. It is, once again, an impulse of energy and information.

In other words, at a preverbal level, all of nature speaks the same language. We are all thinking bodies in a thinking universe. And just as thought projects itself as the molecules of our body, so too the same impulses of energy and information project themselves as space-time events in our environment.

Behind the visible garment of the universe, beyond the mirage of molecules, the *maya* — or illusion — of physicality, lies an inherently invisible, seamless matrix made up of a nothingness. This invisible nothingness silently orchestrates, instructs, guides, governs, and compels nature to express itself with infinite creativity, infinite abundance, and unfaltering exactitude into a myriad of designs and patterns and forms.

Life experiences are the continuum in this seamless matrix of nothingness, in this continuum of both body and environment. They are our experiences of joy and sorrow, of success and failure, of wealth and poverty. All these events seemingly happen to us, but at very primordial levels *we are making them happen.*

The impulses of energy and information that create our life experiences are reflected in our attitudes toward life. And our attitudes are an outcome of and expressions of self-engendered impulses of energy and information.

CHAPTER 2

The A-to-Z Steps to a Richer Life

What then are the states of
awareness, the information and energy states that give rise
to the experience of wealth in our lives? For the sake of
convenience, and to make it easy to remember, I have listed
them in order as the A-to-Z steps to a richer life.

In my experience, it is not necessary to *consciously*
practice the attitudes I am about to describe in order to
materialize wealth. Using effort to consciously practice an
attitude or to cultivate a mood is unnecessary and can cause
stress and strain. It is important only that we know what
these A-to-Z attitudes are, that we know what the steps are,

that we be *aware* of them. The more we become aware of them, the more this knowledge gets structured in our consciousness and awareness. Then it is more likely that our attitude and behavior will change spontaneously, without any effort on our part.

Knowledge has organizing power inherent in it. It is simply enough to know, to be aware of the principles; the knowledge will be processed and metabolized by our bodies, and the results will be spontaneous. The results do not occur overnight, but begin to manifest gradually over a period of time.

If you will look at this list and read it once a day or listen to it on tape every day, then you will see the changes that happen spontaneously in your life and the effortless ease with which wealth and affluence come into your life.

. . . .

*stands for all possibili-*ties, absolute, authority, affluence, and abundance. The true nature of our ground state and that of the universe is that it is a field of all possibilities. In our most primordial form, we are a field of all possibilities.

From this level it is possible to create anything. This field is our own essential nature. It is our inner self.

It is also called the absolute, and it is the ultimate authority. It is intrinsically affluent because it gives rise to the infinite diversity and abundance of the universe.

. . . .

B *stands for better and best.*
Evolution implies getting better and better in every way
with time, ultimately getting for ourselves the best of
everything. People with wealth consciousness settle only
for the best. This is also called the principle of highest first.
Go first class all the way and the universe will respond by
giving you the best.

. . . .

C

stands for carefreeness and charity. A billion dollars in the bank, without the experience of carefreeness and charity, is a state of poverty. Wealth consciousness, by definition, is a state of mind. If you are constantly concerned about how much money you need, then irrespective of the actual dollar amount you have in your account, you are really poor. Carefreeness automatically leads to charity and sharing because the source from which it all comes is infinite, unbounded, and inexhaustible.

. . . .

D *stands for the law of* demand and supply. Whatever service we are here to give, there is a demand for it. Ask yourself "How may I serve?" and "How can I help?" The answers are within you. When you find those answers, you will also see and know that there is a demand for your service.

"D" also stands for *dharma*. Each of us has a dharma, a purpose in life. When we are in dharma, we enjoy and love our work.

. . . .

E *stands for exulting in the*
success of others, especially your competitors and those who
consider themselves your enemies. Your competitors and
enemies will become your helpers when you exult in their
success.

"E" also stands for the principle that expectancy deter-
mines outcome. So always expect the best and you'll see that
the outcome is spontaneously contained in the expectation.

. . . .

F *stands for the fact that in* every failure is the seed of success. In the manifestation of the material from the non-material, of the visible from the invisible, a fundamental mechanics is involved. This is the principle of feedback.

Our failures are stepping-stones in the mechanics of creation, bringing us ever closer to our goals. In reality, there is no such thing as failure. What we call failure is just a mechanism through which we can learn to do things right.

. . . .

G *stands for gratitude,* generosity, God, gap, and goal. Gratitude and generosity are natural attributes of an affluent consciousness. Since the only thing to go after is the best, the principle of the highest first, why not adopt God as the role model? After all, no one is more affluent than God, for God is the field of all possibilities. There is a precise mechanism through which all desires can be manifested. These four steps are as follows:

Step one: You slip into the gap between thoughts. The gap is the window, the corridor, the transformational vortex through which the personal psyche communicates with the cosmic psyche.

Step two: You have a clear intention of a clear goal in the gap.

Step three: You relinquish your attachment to the outcome, because chasing the outcome or getting attached to it entails coming out of the gap.

Step four: You let the universe handle the details.

It is important to have a clear goal in your awareness, but it is also important to relinquish your attachment to the goal. And the goal is in the gap, and the gap is the potentiality to organize and orchestrate the details required to affect any outcome.

Perhaps you recall an instant when you were trying to remember a name, and you struggled and struggled, but with no success. Finally, you let go of your attachment to the outcome, and then a little while later the name flashed across the screen of your consciousness. This is the mechanics for the fulfillment of any desire.

When you were struggling to recall the name, the mind was very active and turbulent. But ultimately, out of fatigue and frustration, you let go and the mind became quiet and slowly quieter — perhaps so quiet that it was almost still — and you slipped into the gap where you released your desire, and soon it was handed to you. This is the true meaning of "Ask and you shall receive," or "Knock and the door shall be opened to you."

One of the easiest and most effortless ways of slipping into the gap is through the process of meditation. And there are many forms of meditation and prayer that can help us to manifest desires from the level of the gap.

.   .   .   .

H *stands for happiness* and humanity and the fact that we are here to make all humans we come into contact with happy. Life naturally evolves in the direction of happiness. We must constantly ask ourselves if what we are doing is going to make us, and those around us, happy. Because happiness is the ultimate goal. It is the goal of all other goals. When we seek money, or a good relationship, or a great job, what we are really seeking is happiness. The mistake we make is not going for happiness first. If we did, everything else would follow.

. . . .

I *stands for the power of* unbending intent or intention. It is to make an unchangeable decision from which it is impossible to go back. It is singlemindedness of purpose. It is a well-defined purpose not countermanded by any other conflicting desires or interests. In order to acquire wealth — or for that matter, anything in the physical universe — you must intend it, make a decision to go for it. The decision is unchangeable with fixity of purpose, not countermanded by anything. The universe handles the details, organizes and orchestrates opportunities. You have simply to be alert to these opportunities.

· · · · · · · · · ·

J *stands for the fact that it* is not necessary to judge. When we relinquish our need to constantly classify things as good or bad, right or wrong, then we experience more silence in our consciousness. Our internal dialogue begins to quieten when we shed the burden of judgment, and it is then easier to access the gap.

It is important, therefore, to get away from definitions, labels, descriptions, interpretations, evaluations, analyses, and judgment, for all of these create the turbulence of our internal dialogue.

. . . .

K *stands for the fact that* organizing power is inherent in knowledge. Knowledge of any kind gets metabolized spontaneously and brings about a change in awareness from where it is possible to create new realities. For example, becoming familiar with the knowledge in this book will spontaneously create the conditions for wealth and affluence.

. . . .

L *stands for love and luxury.*
Love yourself. Love your customers. Love your family. Love everybody. Love the world. There is no power stronger than love.

Also, adopt luxury as a lifestyle. Luxury is our natural state. Adopting luxury as a lifestyle sets the preamble, the preconditions for the flow of wealth.

. . . .

 *stands for making*
money for others and helping others make money. Help-
ing others make money and helping other people to fulfill
their desires is a sure way to ensure you'll make money for
yourself as well as more easily fulfill your own dreams.

"M" also stands for motivate. The best way to motivate other people to help you fulfill your goals is to help
them fulfill their goals.

. . . .

N *stands for saying no to* negativity. My friend Wayne Dyer, the famous author, taught me a simple technique for this. Whenever he has a negative thought he silently says to himself, "Next" and moves on.

Saying no to negativity also means not being around negative people. Negative people deplete your energy. Surround yourself with love and nourishment and do not allow the creation of negativity in your environment.

. . . .

O *stands for the fact that* life is the coexistence of all opposite values. Joy and sorrow, pleasure and pain, up and down, hot and cold, here and there, light and darkness, birth and death. All experience is by contrast, and one would be meaningless without the other.

A wise seer once said, "A man born blind from birth will never know the meaning of darkness because he has never experienced light."

When there is a quiet reconciliation, an acceptance in our awareness of this lively coexistence of all opposite values, then automatically we become more and more nonjudgmental. The victor and the vanquished are seen as two poles of the same being. Nonjudgment leads to quietening of the internal dialogue, and this opens once again the doorway to creativity.

"O" also stands for opportunity and open and honest communication. Every contact with every human being is an opportunity for growth and the fulfillment of desire — one has only to be alert to the opportunities through increased awareness. Open and honest communication opens the channels to realize those opportunities.

. . . .

P *stands for purpose in life* and for pure potentiality. We are here to fulfill a purpose. It is up to us to find out what that purpose is. Once we know our purpose then the knowledge of one's purpose leads to the insight that we are true potentiality.

We must be able to state our purpose in very simple terms. For example, my purpose in life is to heal, to make everyone I come into contact with happy, and to create peace.

Knowing our purpose opens up the doorway to the field of pure potentiality because inherent in our desire are the seeds and mechanics for its fulfillment. The Vedic seer states, "I am the immeasurable potential of all that was, is, and will be, and my desires are like seeds left in the ground:

they wait for the right season and then spontaneously manifest into beautiful flowers and mighty trees, into enchanted
gardens and majestic forests."

. . . .

Q *is to question: to question* dogma, question ideology, question outside authority. It is only by questioning what people take for granted, what people hold to be true, that we can break through the hypnosis of social conditioning.

. . . .

R *stands for the fact that*
receiving is as necessary as giving. To graciously receive is
an expression of the dignity of giving. Those who are un-
able to receive are actually incapable of giving. Giving and
receiving are different aspects of the flow of energy in the
universe.

Giving and receiving do not have to be in the form of
material things. To graciously receive a compliment or admiration or respect also implies the ability to be able to
give these to others. And absence of respect, courtesy, man-
ners, or admiration creates a state of poverty irrespective
of the amount of money you have in the bank.

. . . .

S *stands for spending and* service. Money is like blood; it must flow. Hoarding and holding on to it causes sludging. In order to grow, it must flow. Otherwise it gets blocked and, like clotted blood, it can only cause damage.

Money is life energy that we exchange and use as a result of the service we provide to the universe. And in order to keep it coming to us, we must keep it circulating.

. . . .

T *stands for transcendence,* timeless awareness, talent bank, and tithing. My personal experience is that without transcendence, life has no beauty. In order to live a full life it is necessary to go beyond all boundaries. As the Sufi poet Rumi has said, "Out beyond ideas of right-doing and wrong-doing there is a field. I'll meet you there." I feel that my experience of transcendence through the practice of meditation gives me an inner stability and silence that is not overshadowed by any activity. That silence stays with me so that no outer experience can overshadow the awareness and experience of the self.

"T" also stands for timeless awareness, as opposed to time-bound awareness. Time-bound awareness occurs when we relinquish the self for the self-image. The self-image is the social mask, the protective veneer behind which we hide. In time-bound awareness our behavior is always influenced by the past and by anticipation and fear of the future. Time-bound awareness is burdened by guilt and sorrow. It is rooted in fear. It causes entropy, aging, and death. Timeless awareness is the awareness of the self.

The Vedic seer says, "I do not worry about the past and I am not fearful of the future because my life is supremely concentrated in the present, and the right response comes to me, to every situation as it occurs." This is also the state of bliss. The self is not in the realm of thought. It's in the gap between our thoughts. The cosmic psyche whispers to us softly in the gap between our thoughts. This is also what we call intuition. Time-bound awareness is in the intellect; it calculates. Timeless awareness is in the heart; it feels.

"T" also stands for talent bank. In order to maximize creativity and offer the best service, it is good to develop a talent bank or a coterie of individuals with unique and diverse talents and abilities and whose individual talents, when added together, are more than the sum of the parts.

"T" also stands for tithing. Tithing means giving away a certain portion of your income without conditions or strings attached. When you give, a vacuum is created that attracts even more of what you have given away. As Emerson said, "Without a rich heart, wealth is an ugly beggar."

. . . .

U

stands for understanding the unity behind all diversity. Unity consciousness is a state of enlightenment where we pierce the mask of illusion which creates separation and fragmentation. Behind the appearance of separation is one unified field of wholeness. Here the seer and the scenery are one.

We experience unity consciousness when we are in love, when we are with nature gazing at the stars or walking on the beach, listening to music, dancing, reading poetry, praying, and in the silence of meditation. In unity consciousness, we slip through the barrier of time into the playground of eternity, as when we say, "The beauty of the mountain was breathtaking; time stood still." Then you and the mountain become one. At a very deep level of awareness, we know that you and I and the mountain and everything else is the same Being in different disguises. This is the state of love — not as a sentiment, but as the ultimate truth, at the heart of all creation.

. . . .

V *stands for values: truth, integrity,* honesty, love, faith, devotion, and beauty. The great Indian poet Rabindranath Tagore says, "When we feel beauty, we know it as truth." Without values, there is confusion and chaos. When values disintegrate everything disintegrates. Health disintegrates, poverty attains dominance over affluence, societies and civilizations crumble. When we pay attention to these values that society has always held sacred, then order emerges out of chaos, and the field of pure potentiality inside us becomes all-powerful, creating anything it desires.

. . . .

W *stands for wealth con-* sciousness without worries. Wealth consciousness implies absence of money worries. Truly wealthy people never worry about losing their money because they know that wherever money comes from there is an inexhaustible supply of it.

Once, when we were discussing a world peace project with Maharishi Mahesh Yogi, somebody asked him, "Where is all the money going to come from?" And he replied without hesitation, "From wherever it is at the moment."

. . . .

X _stands for expressing_ honest appreciation and thanks to all who help us. We must never pretend appreciation, but if we feel it, then we must express it. The expression of gratitude is a powerful force that generates even more of what we have already received.

. . . .

Y *stands for youthful vigor.*
We experience health when our identity of who we are comes from reference to the self. When we identify with objects, whether these are situations, circumstances, people, or things, then we relinquish our energy to the object of reference. As a result, we feel lack of energy and vitality. When our identity comes from the self, then we keep our energy to ourselves. We feel energetic, we feel powerful, and we experience youthful vigor.

. . . .

Z stands for zest for life. It is to appreciate life in all its vitality and exuberance. It is to know that there is only one life that expresses itself in myriad forms. To see that life is to know that power is in the present moment. It is to know that I am that, that you are that, that all this is that, and that's all there is.

Tagore once said, "The same stream of life that runs through the world runs through my veins night and day and dances in rhythmic measure. It is the same life that shoots in joy through the dust of the earth into number-less blades of grass and breaks into tumultuous waves of flowers." He calls this "the life throb of ages, dancing in my blood this moment." To be in touch with this life throb of ages dancing in our blood this moment, is to have zest for life. It is to face the unknown with carefreeness and freedom.

The unknown is the field of all possibilities in every moment of the present. And this is freedom, beyond the known of past conditioning, beyond the prison of space, time, and causation. As Don Juan once said to Carlos Castaneda, "It does not matter what our specific fate is, as long as we face it with ultimate abandon." This is carefreeness. This is joy. This is freedom. This is zest for life.

. . . .

So there you are. These are the stepping-stones to unlimited wealth, the A-to-Z of prosperity. Once again, you do not need to consciously cultivate a mood of these attributes. You need only to be aware of them. Read the list daily, or just listen to it on tape, and you will see your life change and become an expression of affluence, of unboundedness, abundance, infinity, and immortality.

Create as much wealth as your heart desires. Fulfill every material and nonmaterial desire. Create wealth and spend it. Spend it lavishly and then share it and give it to others. Give it to your children, to your family, to your relatives, to your friends, to society, and to the world. For wealth is of the universe and it does not belong to us — we belong to it.

We are privileged children and the universe has chosen to share its bounty with us. We only have to give our attention to affluence and it will be ours. Attention is all that counts. A great seer from India once said, "You are where your attention takes you. In fact, you are your attention. If your attention is fragmented, you are fragmented.

When your attention is in the past, you are in the past. When your attention is in the present moment, you are in the presence of God and God is present in you."

Simply be aware of the present, of what you are doing. The presence of God is everywhere, and you have only to consciously embrace it with your attention.

Let the waters settle
you will see stars and moon
mirrored in your Being.

— Rumi

PART II

Wealth Consciousness
in the Field of All Possibilities

CHAPTER 3

The Magic of Attention

*S*o far, we have discussed the steps to affluence in a more or less materialistic sense. But material wealth or money is merely one means to the spontaneous fulfillment of our desires.

Affluence or wealth means that one is easily able to fulfill one's desires, whatever they may be, whether they apply to the material realm, or to our emotional, psychological or spiritual needs, or to the realm of relationship.

A truly wealthy person's attention is never focused on money alone. Moreover, a wealthy person never has money concerns. You may have millions of dollars in the bank, but if you think all the time about money, if you have concern about it, if you worry about it — about getting more, about not having enough, about losing it — then irrespective of the dollar amount you possess, you are poor. As Oscar Wilde once said, "There is only one class of people that thinks more about money than the rich, and that is the poor. In fact, the poor can think of nothing else."

To have true wealth or affluence is to be totally care-free about everything in life, including money. True wealth consciousness is, therefore, consciousness of the source of all material reality. This source of all material reality is pure consciousness. It is pure awareness. It is the unified field. It is the field of all possibilities. We cannot know this field just by thinking about it because, by definition, it is transcendental to thought. We can, however, have experiential knowledge of this field by transcending to it and knowing it intimately as our own nature.

When we transcend, we know nonverbally without the use of words. We obtain knowledge directly, without the distracting intervention of spoken language. This is the value of meditation, which gives us the experience of pure

Being, although the experience of pure Being is in itself an expression of pure bliss and pure joy. The main advantage of alternating the experience of meditation with activity is that the more we dive into the field of pure Being, pure awareness, pure consciousness, the more our activity becomes infused with it. And then our activity acquires the qualities inherent in pure Being, in pure consciousness: infinite, unbounded, abundant, affluent, and immortal.

The best way to acquire knowledge of this field of pure Being is through meditation. Knowing about the qualities intellectually and putting attention on the qualities also helps, because, ultimately, whatever we experience is a result of the quality of our attention.

. . . .

In this chapter I would like to explain once more in a little detail the quantum field.

Physicists tell us that as we go beyond the realm of subatomic particles into the cloud of subatomic particles which makes up the atom, which makes up everything in reality, that when we try to examine and understand these particles — which have fancy names like quarks and bosons and leptons, and so on — these particles are so small that we can never measure them. There are no instruments that are available or will ever be available that will measure the minute smallness of these particles. In fact, they are so small that we can only *think* about them.

Now, there is another very interesting fact about these particles: they have never been seen. So, if you can't observe these subatomic particles, if you can't see them, how do we even know that they exist? And the answer is, we know that they exist by the evidence of the trails they leave behind in particle accelerators. In places where they are doing research on subatomic theory, one can see — and even photograph — the trails that these particles leave behind. And by looking at the trails, one knows that they did, in fact, exist. But there is another very interesting facet to these particles, and that is that they come into existence only when we observe them.

So, if we are looking at a quantum field, every time we look at it these particles blink into existence. And every time we turn our attention away from them they disappear into a void. They blink on and off like little lights in a dark room. The dark room you can imagine as infinite, unbounded space, and the particles that blink into existence do so by the mere act of putting attention on the field. When you put your attention on the field, then they come into existence. When you're not putting your attention on the field, then they are just a probability amplitude in the field of all possibilities.

Each particle is a wave at the same time. And it's a wave until the moment of observation. A wave is not restricted to any one location in space or time; a wave is a diffuse thing. That's why it's called a probability amplitude in the field of all possibilities. It defines the statistical likelihood of finding a particle at a certain place at the time of observation — which means the time of attention.

It is attention that transforms the probability amplitude, the wave, the probability distribution, for a possible measurement as a function of time. Attention takes that probability amplitude and brings it into material existence just by the mere act of observation, and the mere act of observation is, of course, putting our attention on it. So, a particle is literally created by you and me through the act of observation. Before it was observed it was just a mathematical possibility, a probability distribution for a possible measurement as a function of time.

THE MAGIC OF ATTENTION

Before observation

∿ Wave

Spread out over space and time

(probability amplitude)

Non-material, non-local

In the realm of the mind

At time of observation

● Particle

Space-time event

Localized

In the realm of the material

Just see how magical this is! It is the quality of our attention that is bringing a certain probability amplitude in the field of infinite possibilities into material existence. In fact, all of material creation is nothing but the self experiencing itself through different qualities of its own attention to itself. If our attention is fragmented, then we are fragmented. If our attention is on wholeness, we are wholeness.

The Vedic seers say, "Have your attention on what is and see its fullness in every moment. The presence of God is everywhere. You have only to consciously embrace it with your attention."

CHAPTER 4

The Power of Knowledge, Desire, and Spirit

Let's examine the qualities of the unified field, the self, pure Being, which is the source of all abundance and affluence in the universe. After all, if we were to choose a role model, if we were to choose something that we must emulate, why not choose the unified field, the source of all creation, as our role model?

The following twenty-five qualities are ascribed to the unified field. This list was developed several years ago, when Maharishi Mahesh Yogi, the founder of the Transcendental Meditation technique, asked a group of physicists to describe the qualities of the unified field. As it turns out, these are also the qualities of Brahman, the source of all creation as described in the *Veda*, the classic spiritual text of India. If we could think of a person who embodied the thoughts of God, then these would be His or Her psychological traits. And what could be better than to use for our model the mind of God, the unified field, the field of all possibilities? Einstein once said, "I want to know the thoughts of God; the rest are details." So let's examine the qualities of the unified field. And these are:

1

Total potential of natural law.

This means all the laws of nature that are structured, that create the infinite diversity of creation, are found here in the unified field. Today, scientists tell us that there are four basic forces in nature. These are gravity, which makes the earth go 'round and holds the planets together; electromagnetism, which is responsible for light, heat, electricity, all the things that we experience in daily life as energy; the strong interaction that holds the nucleus of an atom together; and the weak interaction that is responsible for

transmutation of elements and radioactive decay. Everything in material creation comes from these four forces. But these aren't merely forces — these are fields of intelligence as well, because the ultimate ground of these forces, the unified field, is a field of infinite, unbounded intelligence, and is therefore the total potential of natural law.

2

Infinite organizing power.

The field is organizing everything in creation: the movement of galaxies, the movement of stars, the rotation of the earth, the cycles of the seasons, the biological rhythms of our bodies, birds migrating at the right season to the right place, fish returning to their spawning grounds, the biological rhythms of nature as found in flowers, vegetation, and animals. It is literally a field of infinite organizing power. It can do an infinite number of things all at the same time and then correlate them with each other.

Even our human body is a field of infinite organizing power. There are six trillion reactions occurring in the

human body every second, and every one of them is corre-
lated with every single other reaction; every single other
biochemical event knows what other biochemical event is
occurring in the body. A human body can think thoughts,
play a piano, sing a song, digest food, eliminate toxins, kill
germs, monitor the movement of stars, and make a new
baby all at the same time, and correlate each of these activities with every other activity. So, inherent in the field
itself is infinite organizing power. To know that field intimately, to have experiential knowledge of that field as one's
own nature, is to automatically embody the infinite organizing power of the field.

3

Fully awake within itself.

It is the field of pure awareness. It is pure wakefulness.
It is lively. It is not dormant. Even though it is silent, it is
fully awake. In that field of pure awareness, any eventuality
is possible through the quality of the attention in the field
itself.

4

Infinite correlation.

Again, correlating everything with everything else.

5

Perfect orderliness.

The field is one of order. In other words, there is perfect order, even though on the surface it may appear chaotic. Recently there has been a lot of information on so-called chaos theory, which simply means that even though the surface implies chaos, deep within the chaos is an order.

Let's say you went to New York City and you happened to be at Grand Central Station, and if you were to look from the outside at what was happening, you'd see that there is a tremendous amount of chaos. People are rushing here, there, everywhere, and there seemingly is no order. But, of course, every person is going to a specific destination. And, therefore, underlying that seeming disorder is, in fact, a very orderly state existing.

Let's say that at the last moment somebody announced

a track change — train X, instead of leaving from track eleven, is going to leave from track twelve. Now, you'd see even more chaos. You'd see that people are now quickly changing their direction and going hither and thither and rushing; but, in fact, there is order underneath, there's a definite purpose to all that activity.

There is order as well to the unified field because it is organizing an infinite number of things all at the same time. On the surface, it can appear very chaotic and can even lead to seemingly chaotic activity and seemingly chaotic thinking. But there's an underlying order behind that.

6

Infinite dynamism.

The field is dynamic. Even though it is silent, it has the infinite dynamism that can create any possibility. The field is fluid; it is flexible. The flexibility is an aspect of its unmanifest nature. It is silent. In the silence is the source of the dynamism just as in rest is the potential for activity. The deeper the silence, the more the dynamism.

7

Infinite creativity.

After all, what could be more creative than the act of manifesting the entire universe? But the manifestation of the universe is nothing other than the manifestation of thought from the level of Being. Pure Being, thinking to itself, "May I become the waters," becomes the waters. Thinking to itself, "May I become the mountains," becomes the mountains; "May I become the galaxies," becomes the galaxies. Pure Being, undisturbed, silent, eternal, is the state of bliss. A flicker of thought in this state, a little disturbance, and out of it the whole universe manifests.

The great Sufi poet Rumi, once said, "We come spinning out of nothingness, scattering stars like dust." This is the mechanics of creation.

8

Pure knowledge.

Pure knowledge is not knowledge about this or that, it's knowledge about everything that exists in material creation. It is the potentiality, the immeasurable potential of all that was, all that is, all that will be.

9

Unboundedness.

The unified field is not constrained by boundaries, conceptual notions, or premature cognitive commitments. The field is unbounded in space and time. It has no limits in time; it is eternal. It has no limits in space; it is beyond the outer edges of space.

10

Perfect balance.

The field balances everything in creation — the ecology of nature, the physiology of the human body, the evolution of a human fetus into a baby.

11

Self-sufficiency.

The unified field requires nothing from the outside

because everything is contained in the inside of the field. Curving back within itself, it creates again and again.

12

All possibilities.

This means *all* possibilities — *anything* that you can imagine, and more. Therefore you have the ability to acquire anything that falls within the realm of your imagination, and even those things that are currently outside the limits of your imagination. The more you acquire, the more your imagination will expand. What is unimaginable today might become imaginable tomorrow. But there will always be new realms that have yet to be explored.

13

Infinite silence.

Infinite silence is the mind of God. It is a mind that can create anything out of the field of pure potentiality. Infinite silence contains infinite dynamism. Practice silence and you will acquire silent knowledge.

In this silent knowledge is a computing system that is far more precise and far more accurate and far more powerful than anything that is contained in the boundaries of rational thought.

14

Harmonizing.

The universe is the harmonious interaction of all the elements and forces that create balance and harmony. The word *universe* literally means "one song" (*uni*: one; *verse*: song). In this song, in this harmony, there is peace, laughter, joy, and bliss.

15

Evolutionary.

Everything in nature is evolving to a higher level of existence. Even without trying or thinking, just by virtue of our existence itself, we are evolving to a higher level of awareness. When we are aware of this, we evolve even faster.

16

Self-referral.

The unified field doesn't refer to any outside object in order to know itself, it just goes back within itself to know itself.

17

Invincibility.

The field is indestructible. Fire cannot burn it, water cannot wet it, wind cannot dry it, and weapons cannot cleave it. It is ancient, it is unborn, it never dies.

18

Immortality.

Therefore, it is immortal.

19

Unmanifest.

Even though it is the source of everything in creation that is manifest, by itself it is unmanifest.

20

Nourishing.

The unified field nourishes everything in creation, from a tree to the movement of stars and galaxies, to the migration of birds, to the movement of our own immune system, to the digestive process that is taking place inside us, to the beating of our heart. All this is nourished.

21

Integrating.

Not only does it nourish all these activities, it integrates each with everything else.

22

Simplicity.

And yet its nature is pure simplicity. It's not complicated. Because at the most unmanifest level it is nothing but our own awareness — the *simplest* form of our own awareness.

23

Purifying.

The field purifies everything that it comes into contact with. To purify means to restore something to its original, pristine state. The universe, being the expression of exquisite balance, has its source in purity; therefore the field, which is the source of everything, purifies everything that it comes into contact with.

24

Freedom.

Freedom is inherent in the unified field, and when we contact that field then freedom comes to us. It is freedom that comes from the experiential knowledge of one's real nature. And our real nature is that we are the joyful, silent witness, the nonattached, immortal spirit that animates all manifestation. And to have the experience of that silent witness is to just Be.

This is real freedom — the ability to enjoy the choices we make in every successive moment of the present. It is the ability to spontaneously put our attention on those choices that bring joy to us and also to others.

25

Bliss.

The last quality of the unified field — and the most important — is bliss. Bliss should not be confused with happiness. Happiness is always for a reason. You are happy when someone pays you a compliment, or when you get a great job, or when you make a lot of money, or when you have a satisfying relationship. But when you are happy for no reason whatsoever, in the mere fact of existence, you are in a state of bliss. This bliss is where we come from; it is the nature of existence itself. It is inherent in the field; it is more primordial than our body, nearer to us than our mind. And it follows us wherever we go.

In this state of pure bliss is the expression of pure love. When love is pure you become the embodiment of love. This love is offered to none, denied to none. It just radiates from you, like light from a bonfire or dreams from a dreamer. It kindles the spark of love wherever it falls.

. . . .

How do we embody in our own awareness these qualities of the unified field? There are two ways. One is to be aware of them, and I would suggest taking one quality each day of the month and just having our attention on it.

Remember, attention brings the particle into existence out of a probability amplitude, out of a field of all possibilities. Attention is the very mechanics of precipitating a space-time event in the field of all possibilities. So when we put our attention on that particular quality of the field, it brings it not only into our awareness, but into our life in its material expression.

Scientists have shown that mental events transform themselves into molecules. These molecules are literally messengers from inner space. They are the equivalent of thought. When they were first discovered, they were called neuropeptides because they were initially found in the brain. Now we know that these neuropeptides are not confined to the brain, but permeate every cell in the body. To think a thought is to practice not only brain chemistry, but body chemistry. Every thought you have, every idea you entertain, sends a chemical message to the core of cellular awareness. Putting attention on a word, which is the symbolic expression of an idea, is therefore magical. It transforms the invisible into the visible.

So pick a theme for each day of the month. There are twenty-five qualities for twenty-five days, and then one could restart with the first theme on day twenty-six. Let's say today's theme is freedom. For today, then, have your attention on that word *freedom*. Remember, the word becomes the flesh. The quantum event becomes the neuropeptide. Don't analyze the word. Don't try to define it. Don't evaluate it. Don't interpret it. Just have your attention on the idea. It will soon embed itself in your awareness, in your consciousness. That will cause a positive transformation in your consciousness that will spontaneously change your physiology, and that change in physiology will spontaneously bring about a change in your life experiences.

A second way to develop a physiology that embodies the qualities of the unified field is to have direct experience of it. This is accomplished through the practice of meditation. Meditation allows the mind to experience more and more abstract levels of the thinking process and, ultimately, to transcend to that most abstract level of awareness, transcendental consciousness, which is the unified field itself. This is the state of pure awareness, pure consciousness. Meditation has been part of the spiritual tradition of almost every culture. My own experiences come from the regular practice of Transcendental Meditation.

There are a number of scientific studies that show the beneficial effects of meditating. Blood pressure comes down. Stress is alleviated. Basal metabolic rate goes down. Insomnia, anxiety, and a number of psychosomatic disorders are relieved and disappear. Moreover, there is increased brain wave coherence, which also improves attention span, creativity, learning ability, and memory retrieval. Also, the effects of meditation last into our daily activity, and soon our activity becomes saturated and influenced by the qualities of the unified field. This is because by experientially knowing something we become it. Once we become it, we begin to embody all its properties.

In Vedic literature, the unified field is referred to as Brahman. And there is a Sanskrit phrase, "*Brahmavit brahmaiv bhavate*," which means to the extent one knows Brahman, one becomes Brahman. Therefore, transcending becomes a very practical procedure — to not only experientially know and understand the qualities of the unified field, but to have their values expressed in our daily life, in all our daily activities.

. . . .

In this book, I have outlined for you the steps to wealth consciousness based on a true understanding of the workings of nature. Oscar Wilde, whom I quoted earlier, once said, "When I was young I used to think that money is the most important thing in life. Now that I'm older I know that it is." It's obvious that Mr. Wilde was being facetious, but if we substitute the word "affluence" for "money," then we'll know the truth of this statement. Affluence includes money but is not just money. It is the abundance, the flow, the generosity of the universe, where every desire we have must come true, because as stated earlier, inherent in having the desire is the mechanics for its fulfillment.

The universe is a big dream machine, churning out dreams and transforming them into reality, and our own dreams are inextricably woven into the overall scheme of things. The mechanics for the fulfillment of these dreams are contained firstly in the power of knowledge, known in ancient India as *gyan shakti*, and secondly, in the power of intention or desire, known in ancient India as *iccha shakti*. But the power of knowledge and the power of intention or desire find their immeasurable strength and potentiality in the power of transcending, known as *atma shakti*. *Atma shakti*, the power of the self, is the power of Brahman, where the infinite organizing power of the universe resides.

The Veda says, "Know that one thing by knowing which

everything else can be known." Know that deep inside you, in the innermost recesses of your heart, are the Goddesses of Knowledge and Wealth. Love them and nurture them, and every desire that you have will spontaneously blossom into form. For these Goddesses have only one desire: And that is to be born.

THE
A–TO–Z STEPS TO
A RICHER LIFE

A

All Possibilities, Absolute, Authority, Affluence, Abundance.

B

Better and Best.

C

Carefreeness and Charity.

D

Demand and Supply, Dharma.

E

Exulting in the Success of Others, Expecting the Best.

F

Failure Contains the Seed of Success.

G

Gratitude, Generosity,
God, Gap, Goal.

H

Happiness and Humanity.

I

Intent or Intention.

J

Judgment is Unnecessary.

K

Knowledge Contains Organizing Power.

L

Love and Luxury.

M

Making Money for Others, Motivating Others.

N

Saying No to Negativity.

O

*Life is the Coexistence of Opposites, Opportunity,
Open and Honest Communication.*

P

Purpose in Life, Pure Potentiality.

Q

To Question.

R

Receiving is as Necessary as Giving.

S

Spending and Service.

T

Transcendence, Timeless Awareness, Talent Bank, Tithing.

U

Understanding the Unity Behind All Diversity.

V

Values.

W

Wealth Consciousness Without Worries.

X

Expressing Honest Appreciation and Thanks to All Who Help Us.

Y

Youthful Vigor.

Z

Zest for Life.

The Twenty-five Qualities of the Unified Field

- 1 -

Total potential of natural law.

- 2 -

Infinite organizing power.

- 3 -

Fully awake within itself.

- 4 -

Infinite correlation.

- 5 -

Perfect orderliness.

– 6 –

Infinite dynamism.

– 7 –

Infinite creativity.

– 8 –

Pure knowledge.

– 9 –

Unboundedness.

– 10 –

Perfect balance.

– 11 –

Self-sufficiency.

– 12 –

All possibilities.

– 13 –

Infinite silence.

– 14 –

Harmonizing.

– 15 –

Evolutionary.

– 16 –

Self-referral.

– 17 –

Invincibility.

– 18 –

Immortality.

– 19 –

Unmanifest.

– 20 –

Nourishing.

– 21 –

Integrating.

– 22 –

Simplicity.

– 23 –

Purifying.

– 24 –

Freedom.

– 25 –

Bliss.

ABOUT THE AUTHOR

Deepak Chopra is a world-renowned leader in the field of mind-body medicine and human potential. He is the bestselling author of *The Seven Spiritual Laws of Success*; *Ageless Body, Timeless Mind*; and *Quantum Healing*, as well as numerous audio and video programs that promote health and well-being. His books have been translated into more than thirty languages and he lectures widely throughout North America, South America, India, Europe, Japan, and Australia. Currently he is the Executive Director of the Chopra Center for Well-Being in La Jolla, California.

ALSO FROM DEEPAK CHOPRA

BOOKS:

The Seven Spiritual Laws of Success (Amber-Allen
    Publishing / New World Library)

The Way of the Wizard (Crown / Harmony)

Ageless Body, Timeless Mind (Crown / Harmony)

Journey into Healing (Crown / Harmony)

Restful Sleep (Crown / Harmony)

Perfect Weight (Crown / Harmony)

Perfect Health (Crown / Harmony)

Perfect Digestion (Crown / Harmony)

The Return of Merlin (Crown / Harmony)

Unconditional Life (Bantam)

Quantum Healing (Bantam)

Creating Health (Houghton Mifflin)

Return of the Rishi (Houghton Mifflin)

The Love Poems of Rumi (edited by Deepak Chopra)
    (Crown / Harmony)

AUDIO CASSETTES:

Creating Affluence

The Seven Spiritual Laws of Success

The Crescent Moon: Prose Poems of Rabindranath Tagore

Escaping the Prison of the Intellect

Sacred Verses, Healing Sounds, Volume I: The Bhagavad Gita

*Sacred Verses, Healing Sounds, Volume II: Hymns of the
    Rig Veda*

Living Beyond Miracles (with Dr. Wayne Dyer)

Living Without Limits (with Dr. Wayne Dyer)

Return of the Rishi

VIDEO CASSETTES:

The Healing Mind — Ancient Wisdom, Modern Insights
    (Quantum Publications, Inc.)

Waking Up the Power Within — The Freedom to Heal
    (Quantum Publications, Inc.)

The Seven Spiritual Laws of Success (Mystic Fire Video)

The Way of the Wizard (Mystic Fire Video)

OTHER AUDIO PROGRAMS:

Magical Mind, Magical Body (Nightingale-Conant)

The Higher Self (Nightingale-Conant)

Unconditional Life (Bantam Audio Publishing)

Gitanjali: Offerings from the Heart (Sound Horizons)

Growing Younger (Audio-Video Program) (Time-Life)

If you would like information on workshops, lectures, or other programs by Deepak Chopra, or to order any of the books and tapes listed above, please contact:

> The Chopra Center at La Costa Resort & Spa
> 2013 Costa del Mar Road
> Carlsbad, CA 92009-6801
> (888) 424-6772

Visit Dr. Chopra's website at http://www.chopra.com

Unleash the Healing Power
of Your Mind

Your mind can create perfect health, increase your energy level, heal illness, erase pain better than drugs, protect you from disease, reverse the aging process, and help you lose weight.

In *Magical Mind, Magical Body* Dr. Deepak Chopra shows you how to tap into this miraculous power and utilize a 6000-year-old secret for better health and increased longevity. By implementing the techniques in this audio program, you can:

- ✦ Have more energy
- ✦ Overcome addictions
- ✦ Eat without gaining weight

- ✦ Free yourself from disease
- ✦ Lower your stress level
- ✦ Access your body's natural pharmacy

To order *Magical Mind, Magical Body*, please contact:

Nightingale-Conant Corporation
7300 N. Lehigh Avenue
Niles, Illinois 60714

Phone: 800-525-9000
Fax: 800-647-9198

ALSO FROM NEW WORLD LIBRARY

Creating True Prosperity by Shakti Gawain. Shakti presents a new definition of prosperity, one that places importance on fulfillment of the heart and soul rather than on monetary gain. She dismantles the cause-and-effect relationship most people construct around money and happiness, without ignoring the important role money plays in our lives.

Visionary Business by Marc Allen. This breakthrough book can show you not only how to envision and create success, but also how to build a truly visionary business: one that supports its employees, its community, and even the environment. Presented in the form of an engaging story, this book is filled with twenty-five concrete principles that show us how to create a visionary business.

How to Think Like a Millionaire by Mark Fisher and Marc Allen. A clear, straightforward book for anyone who has ever wondered what makes a millionaire's mind tick, or who wants to put their own thoughts and attitudes on a similar plane. *How to Think Like a Millionaire* opens the door to a revitalizing, life-changing way of thinking.

The Instant Millionaire by Mark Fisher. Loaded with specific financial advice, this book opens doors to both financial and personal well-being. It shows readers of any age or background how to turn an empty bank account into $1,000,000 within six years.

Message of a Master by John McDonald. This is the story of a seemingly miraculous change that takes place in a man after he meets a true master of life. He learns, and shares with us, teachings that allow him to accomplish anything he desires. Originally written in 1929, this book contains a timeless message for all.

ALSO FROM AMBER–ALLEN PUBLISHING

The Seven Spiritual Laws of Success by Deepak Chopra. In this classic international bestseller, Deepak Chopra distills the essence of his teachings into seven simple, yet powerful principles that can easily be applied to create success in all areas of our lives.

Child of the Dawn by Gautama Chopra. A rich and colorful parable about a young boy's search for meaning and empowerment. Based on the principles from his father's book, *The Seven Spiritual Laws of Success,* this engaging tale is guaranteed to enchant and inspire readers of all ages for generations to come.

The Four Agreements by don Miguel Ruiz. Based on ancient Toltec wisdom, the Four Agreements offer a powerful code of conduct that can rapidly transform our lives to a new experience of freedom, true happiness, and love.

Living Beyond Miracles by Deepak Chopra and Wayne Dyer (Audio). Dr. Chopra and Dr. Dyer collaborate for the first time before a live audience. This dynamic presentation features individual talks by the two men, followed by a fascinating and inspiring conversation between them.

The Nature of Personal Reality by Jane Roberts. Seth explains how the conscious mind directs unconscious activity, and has at its command all the powers of the inner self.

The Oversoul Seven Trilogy by Jane Roberts. The adventures of Oversoul Seven are an intriguing fantasy, a mind-altering exploration of our being, and a vibrant celebration of life.

Seth Speaks by Jane Roberts. In this essential guide to conscious living, Seth clearly and powerfully articulates the concept that we create our own reality according to our beliefs.

This book is copublished by Amber-Allen Publishing and New World Library. To contact either company for more information about their products, please note the addresses below and on the following page.

New World Library is dedicated to publishing books and audio programs that inspire and challenge us to improve the quality of our lives and the world.

For a catalog of our books and audio programs, contact:

New World Library
14 Pamaron Way
Novato, California 94949

Phone: (415) 884-2100
Fax: (415) 884-2199
Email: escort@nwlib.com

Or call toll free: (800) 972-6657
Catalog requests: Ext. 50
Ordering: Ext. 52

Visit our web site at www.newworldlibrary.com

Amber-Allen Publishing is dedicated to bringing a message of love and inspiration to all who seek a higher purpose and meaning in life.

For a catalog of our books and audios, please contact:

Amber-Allen Publishing
Post Office Box 6657
San Rafael, California 94903

Phone: (415) 499-4657

Fax: (415) 499-3174

Email: info@amberallen.com

Or call toll free: (800) 624-8855

Visit our web site at www.amberallen.com